Solar System

Published in 2010 by Kingfisher
This edition published in 2013 by Kingfisher
an imprint of Macmillan Children's Books
a division of Macmillan Publishers Limited
20 New Wharf Road
London N1 9RR
Basingstoke and Oxford
Associated companies throughout the world
www.panmacmillan.com

ISBN 978-0-7534-3721-6

First published as *Kingfisher Young Knowledge: Solar System* in 2006
Additional material produced for Macmillan Children's Books by Discovery Books Ltd

1 3 5 7 9 8 6 4 2
1SPL/0713/WKT/UTD/128MA

A CIP catalogue record for this book is available from the British Library.
Printed in China

Note to readers: the website addresses listed in this book are correct at
the time of going to print. However, due to the ever-changing nature
of the internet, website addresses and content can change. Websites
can contain links that are unsuitable for children. The publisher cannot
be held responsible for changes in website addresses or content, or
for information obtained through a third party. We strongly advise
that internet searches should be supervised by an adult.

Acknowledgements
The publishers would like to thank the following for permission to reproduce their material. Every care has been taken
to trace copyright holders. However, if there have been unintentional omissions or failure to trace copyright holders,
we apologize and will, if informed, endeavour to make corrections in any future edition.
b = bottom, *c* = centre, *l* = left, *t* = top, *r* = right

Pages 4–5 NASA/Corbis; 6–7 NASA/SPL; 8*bl* Getty Images; 8–9 Getty Images; 10*cl* SPL; 10–11 NASA; 11*b* Corbis; 12–13 NASA/Corbis; 13*tl* Corbis;
13*bl* Mary Evans Picture Library; 16 Getty Images; 17*t* Getty Images; 18–19 Corbis; 18*r* NASA; 19*t* Getty Images; 19*b* Getty Images; 20–21 NASA; 21*tr*
NASA; 21*bl* NASA; 22*bl* Galaxy; 22*cr* NASA/SPL; 23*t* Corbis; 23*b* NASA; 24*c* SPL; 24–25 NASA; 25*b* Kobal Collection; 26–27*t* NASA/SPL; 27*cl* NASA/SPL;
27*br* Corbis; 28–29 Corbis; 30*c* SPL; 30–31 Corbis; 31*tr* Corbis; 32–33 NASA/SPL; 33*tr* NASA/SPL; 37*br* NASA/SPL; 38*bl* The Art Archive; 38–39 Corbis;
39*br* Corbis; 40–41*t* Getty Images; 40–41*b* Galaxy Picture Library; 42–43 NASA/Corbis; 47*br* Alamy Images; 48*r* Shutterstock Images/Vladmir Petrov;
48*b* Shutterstock Images/argonaut; 49*c* Shutterstock Images/Giovanni Benintende; 49*b* Shutterstock Images/Sebastian Kaulitzhi; 52*t* Shutterstock
Images/2Happy; 52*b* Shutterstock Images/Herb Sennet; 53*t* Shutterstock Images/Gheorghe Bunescu Bogdan Mircea; 53*l* Shutterstock Images/mashe;
56 Shutterstock Images/iofoto

Commissioned artwork on pages 34–35 and 40–44 by Daniel Shutt; commissioned photography on pages 44–47 by Andy Crawford
Thank you to models Holly Hadaway and Sonnie Nash

Solar System

Dr Mike Goldsmith

KINGFISHER

Contents

Solar System **6**

Round and round **8**

Fiery star **10**

Fast Mercury **12**

Roasting Venus **14**

Our planet Earth **16**

Earth's Moon **18**

Moon visit **20**

Rusty Mars **22**

Living with martians **24**

Giant Jupiter **26**

Ringed Saturn **28**

Cold Uranus **30**

Stormy Neptune **32**

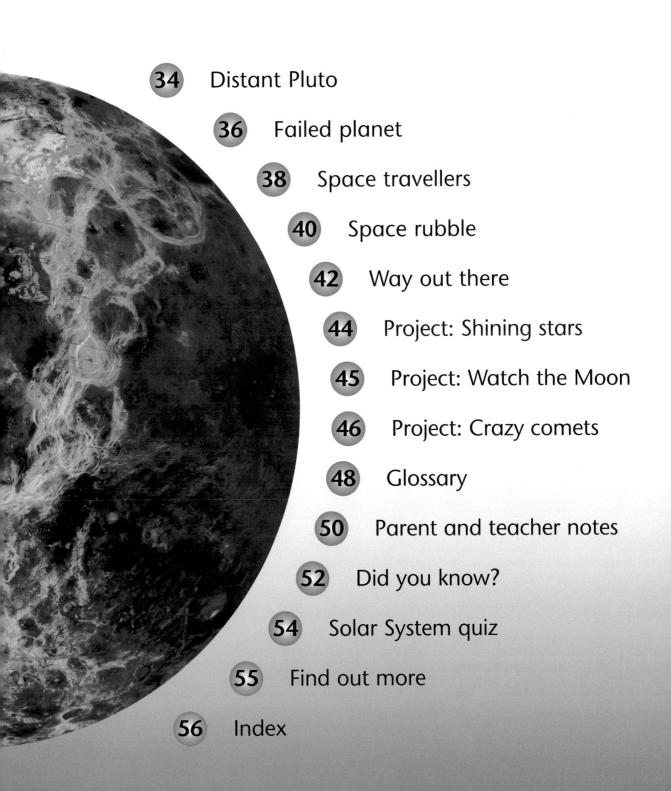

34 Distant Pluto

36 Failed planet

38 Space travellers

40 Space rubble

42 Way out there

44 Project: Shining stars

45 Project: Watch the Moon

46 Project: Crazy comets

48 Glossary

50 Parent and teacher notes

52 Did you know?

54 Solar System quiz

55 Find out more

56 Index

Solar System

The Earth that we live on, the Sun and the Moon are all parts of the Solar System. It is called the Solar System because everything goes around the Sun and solar means 'of the Sun'.

Other worlds

There are eight planets in the Solar System and Earth is just one of them. Most of the planets also have moons going around them. Pluto used to be thought of as a planet. However, astronomers now call it a 'dwarf planet', because it is so small.

Sun

Mars

Earth

Venus

Mercury

Pluto (dwarf planet)

Uranus

Neptune

Saturn

Jupiter

Space rocks

The Sun, planets and moons are not the only things in the Solar System. There are dwarf planets, asteroids, meteoroids, dust and gases too. Comets are like huge, dirty snowballs. Asteroids are giant chunks of rock and meteoroids are small pieces of rock.

Round and round

All eight planets in the Solar System travel through space, going around the Sun. The time that it takes a planet to go around the Sun once is called a year.

The pull of gravity

The force that pulls things towards each other is called gravity. If you throw a football into the air, it is gravity that pulls it down again. The Sun's gravity holds the planets in place. If there was no gravity, the Earth would fall to pieces and you would be thrown into space.

Around the Sun

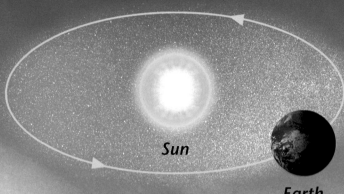

Sun

Earth

Earth goes around the Sun in about 365 days. Planets closer to the Sun have shorter orbits, so they go around it quicker. Mercury's year is 88 days.

Day and night

Each planet also spins around, causing it to have day and night. On other planets, these are not the same length as Earth's. The days on Venus are 243 times longer than ours!

Fiery star

The Sun is the only star in the Solar System. It is so big, Earth could fit into it a million times! The Sun is also very hot – much hotter than an oven.

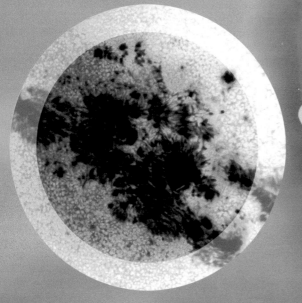

Spotty Sun
The surface of the Sun is constantly moving. Sometimes, dark, cool spots (above) form on the Sun's surface. These spots are called sunspots.

prominence

Great balls of fire

Prominences are giant masses of gas thrown off by the Sun. They look just like the leaping flames of a fire.

Warning! Hot Sun

It is dangerous to look straight at the Sun. When you play in the sunshine, always wear a hat, sunglasses and suncream.

Fast Mercury

Mercury is a small planet that orbits very close to the Sun. The Sun's light makes Mercury's days incredibly hot, but nights on Mercury are bitterly cold – much colder than any freezer. This is because there is no air to stop the heat from escaping.

Rocks galore!

The surface of Mercury is dry and rocky with gigantic cliffs. Mercury also has huge craters (hollows) caused by the fall of rocks millions of years ago.

Mighty Mariner
The spacecraft
Mariner 10 flew past
Mercury three times
in 1974 and 1975.
It took photographs
of about half the planet.

God of speed
According to the myths of
ancient Rome, Mercury
was the messenger of the
gods. He was supposed
to fly quickly because he
had wings on his heels.

Roasting Venus

Venus is the closest planet to Earth. On Venus, the sky is yellow and cloudy. The clouds trap the Sun's heat, which makes Venus a very, very hot planet.

Violent volcanoes

There are massive volcanoes on Venus. Some are much higher than any mountains on Earth. Venus's most famous volcano is called Maat Mons. It is over nine kilometres high. Sometimes on Venus, all the volcanoes erupt together, covering the whole planet in lava.

Lightning strikes
The air on Venus is full of deadly acid, and lightning flickers in the sky. Many spaceships have visited Venus, but they have been destroyed by the heat and acid in the air.

Our planet Earth

Earth is the planet that we live on. Most of its surface is covered with water, so from space, the Earth looks blue. Together, the water, air and warmth of the Sun make life on Earth possible.

Life on Earth

There are over 30 million different types of plants and animals on Earth. They live everywhere, from the deepest ocean to the top of the highest mountain.

dolphins

Restless planet

Compared to the other planets in the Solar System, Earth has many volcanoes and earthquakes. Deep underground, the Earth is so hot that the rock is molten. When a volcano erupts, the molten rock escapes onto the planet's surface.

Earth's Moon

The Moon is our closest neighbour in space. Just as the Earth orbits the Sun, the Moon goes around planet Earth. There is no life or weather on the Moon – no clouds, wind, rain or snow.

Hide and seek

The Moon takes a month to go around the Earth. It also takes a month to spin around. Because of this, we only ever see one side of the Moon from Earth. However, spaceships have travelled around the Moon so we know what the far side looks like.

full Moon

gibbous Moon

last quarter

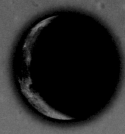
crescent Moon

Changing Moon

As the Moon moves, different parts of it are lit by the Sun. This makes it look as if the Moon is changing shape. The different shapes are called phases.

Crusty craters

Most of the Moon's craters were made millions of years ago when huge chunks of rock crashed into it.

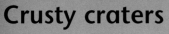

Moon visit

The Moon is the only other world people have visited. On the Moon, astronauts weigh one-sixth as much as at home.

Buzzing around
In 1969, Buzz Aldrin (born 1930) and Neil Armstrong (born 1930) were the first astronauts to land on the Moon. They stayed there for 21 hours before returning to Earth.

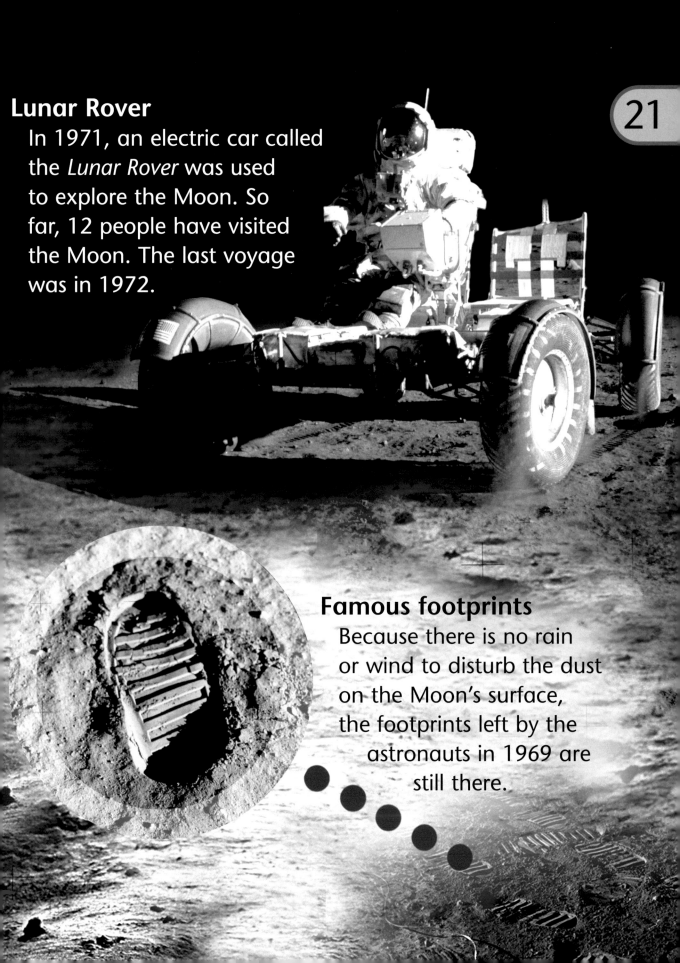

Lunar Rover

In 1971, an electric car called the *Lunar Rover* was used to explore the Moon. So far, 12 people have visited the Moon. The last voyage was in 1972.

Famous footprints

Because there is no rain or wind to disturb the dust on the Moon's surface, the footprints left by the astronauts in 1969 are still there.

Rusty Mars

Mars is red because it is rusty. There is a lot of iron in the soil, and the air on Mars has made it turn red — just like rusty iron on Earth.

Poles of ice

Like Earth, the poles (the top and bottom ends of the planet) of Mars are covered in ice. The ice becomes thicker in winter.

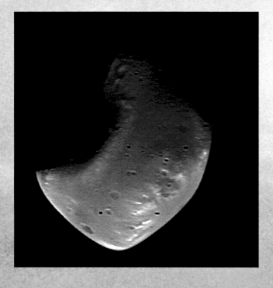

Two moons

Mars has two tiny moons called Phobos (left) and Deimos (above). Phobos is moving closer and closer to Mars, and scientists think that one day it will crash into Mars.

Mighty Mons

Mars's surface is covered with deserts, canyons, craters and gigantic dead volcanoes. Olympus Mons is the tallest volcano in the Solar System. It is 24 kilometres high.

Living with martians

Long ago, the air on Mars was thicker, and there were valleys filled with water. This means that there may have been life on the red planet.

Super Spirit

In 2004, *Spirit* landed on Mars after a seven-month journey through space. It sent pictures of Mars back to Earth, and studied the soil and rocks there.

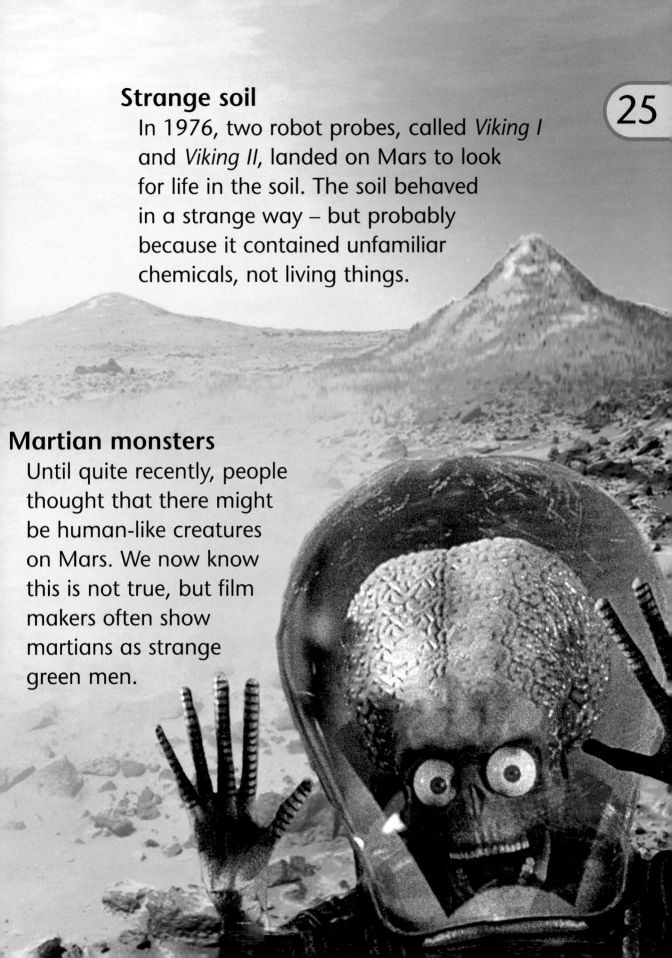

Strange soil

In 1976, two robot probes, called *Viking I* and *Viking II*, landed on Mars to look for life in the soil. The soil behaved in a strange way – but probably because it contained unfamiliar chemicals, not living things.

Martian monsters

Until quite recently, people thought that there might be human-like creatures on Mars. We now know this is not true, but film makers often show martians as strange green men.

Giant Jupiter

Jupiter is the biggest planet. It is 1,300 times the size of Earth. It spins around quickly, so its days are only ten hours long. Because it does not have a solid surface, it is impossible to land a spaceship on Jupiter.

Huge red spot
Jupiter is a very stormy planet. One storm has already lasted for over 300 years! From the Earth, this storm looks like a giant red spot.

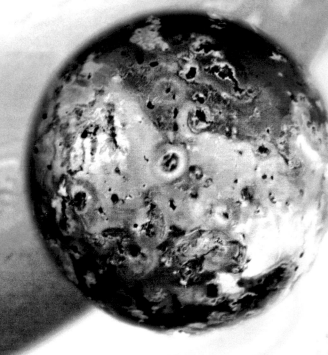

Marvellous moons

Jupiter has many moons. The moon shown here, Io, has active volcanoes. Europa has an icy surface and Ganymede is the biggest moon in the Solar System – it is bigger than the planet Mercury.

Great Galileo

In 1609, using a home-made telescope, the Italian scientist Galileo Galilei (1564–1642) discovered four of Jupiter's moons.

Ringed **Saturn**

Many people think that
Saturn is the most beautiful
world in the Solar System. Saturn
is so light that if there were an ocean
big enough, the planet would float in it.

Rings of rock

Saturn's rings are made of billions of
pieces of rocks and dust. Although the
planets Jupiter, Uranus and Neptune
also have ring systems, theirs
are not as bright or as
big as Saturn's.

Studying Saturn

The *Cassini* probe was launched in 1997 on a mission to study Saturn, its rings and its moons. *Cassini* arrived in 2004.

Cold Uranus

Uranus is a huge, cold, blue-green world far out in space. It is surrounded by many black rings and icy moons. Because of the odd way it spins, nights on some parts of Uranus can last for more than 40 years.

Twisted Miranda

The surface of Miranda, one of Uranus's moons, is incredibly twisted and jumbled. It has cliffs over 20 kilometres high, enormous ridges, grooves and craters.

Uranus

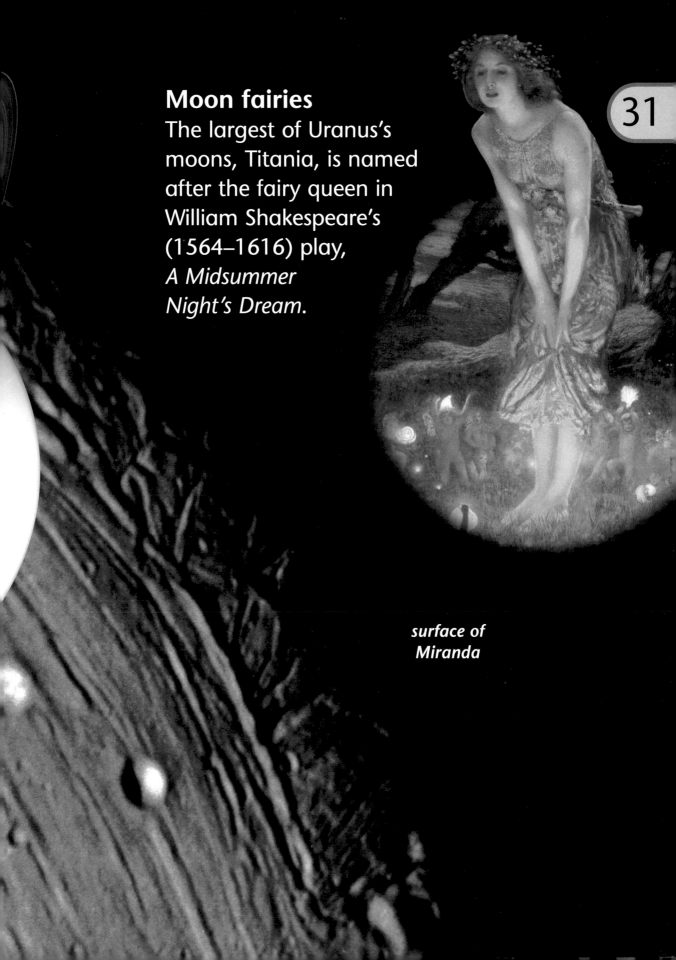

Moon fairies

The largest of Uranus's moons, Titania, is named after the fairy queen in William Shakespeare's (1564–1616) play, *A Midsummer Night's Dream*.

surface of Miranda

Stormy Neptune

Neptune is an extremely cold, blue world. It is so far away from the Earth that the space probe *Voyager 2* took 12 years to reach it!

Cold volcanoes

This picture shows the surface of Triton, one of Neptune's moons. Triton has great volcanic eruptions of liquid nitrogen.

Stormy clouds

Neptune is the stormiest
planet. The winds there can
blow up to 2,000 kilometres
per hour – three times as
fast as Earth's hurricanes!
Sometimes, storm clouds
appear as white streaks
or dark spots on its
cloudy surface.

Distant **Pluto**

Pluto is called a 'dwarf planet' because it is so small. It is farther from the Sun than the other planets. It is tiny, reddish-brown and smaller than Earth's moon.

Sun

Charon

Colossal Charon

Pluto is so small that it can only be seen from Earth with a powerful telescope. It has a moon called Charon. Charon was discovered only in 1978. It is darker and greyer than Pluto but, like Pluto, it is also covered in rocks and ice.

In the dark

If you visited Pluto, the Sun would look like a bright star. Pluto is so far away from the Sun that it is always dark. No spaceship has reached this dwarf planet, so we do not really know what it looks like.

Pluto

Failed planet

Beyond Mars and Jupiter there are billions of pieces of rock and metal called asteroids. They are much smaller than planets. Scientists believe that the asteroids are pieces of a planet that failed to form.

Asteroid belt

Most asteroids can be found in two regions or 'belts'. One of the belts is between Mars and Jupiter, and the other is beyond Neptune.

Asteroid Ida

Ida is a small, potato-shaped asteroid with its own tiny moon. In 1993 the *Galileo* space probe took pictures of Ida as it flew past.

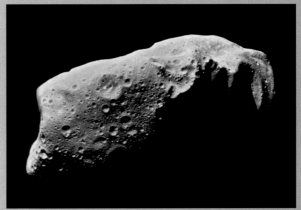

Space travellers

Comets are visitors from the outer parts of the Solar System. They are lumps of ice and dust: a bit like dirty icebergs drifting through space. When the comets are close to the Sun, the ice turns to gas.

Return of the comet

All comets orbit the Sun. Some take hundreds, thousands or even millions of years to return. Halley's comet returns only every 76 years. This famous tapestry shows Halley's comet (top left) in 1066.

Two-tailed Hale-Bopp

As a comet moves closer to the Sun, it forms two tails. One of the tails is made of gas and the other of dust. The gas tail points away from the Sun. In this picture of comet Hale-Bopp, the gas tail is blue and the dust tail is whitish.

Comet crash!

In 1994, pieces of a comet called Shoemaker-Levy 9 broke up and smashed into Jupiter. This left patches in Jupiter's atmosphere that lasted for many months.

Space rubble

There are many pieces of rock and dust drifting in space. These objects are called meteoroids. Many meteoroids are left behind by comets.

Shooting stars!

Every year, 200,000 tonnes of meteoroids fall through the Earth's atmosphere. As large meteoroids rush through the air, they become so hot that they glow. This falling glow is called a meteor or a shooting star.

Huge Hoba

Meteors that land on the
Earth are called meteorites.
The heaviest known meteorite
is Hoba West. It was found
in 1920 in Namibia and
weighs about 60 tonnes –
that is about as heavy
as nine elephants!

Way out there

In 1961, a Russian called Yuri Gagarin (1934–1968) became the first person to journey into space and go right around the Earth. Since then, many astronauts have travelled through space.

Drifting through space

Exploring space is dangerous. Sometimes, astronauts leave their spaceships to 'walk' in space. This astronaut is wearing a device that can push him back to his spaceship if he starts to drift away.

Life in space

In space there is no air, nothing has any weight and there is no 'up' or 'down', which can make life difficult. Some space travellers get space-sick, just like people on Earth get sea-sick.

Shining stars

Bedroom planetarium

Dome-shaped buildings called planetariums have lights that show the night sky. Use a torch to make your own star in the sky.

You will need
- Torch
- Pencil
- Card and sheet of paper
- Pair of scissors
- Sticky tape

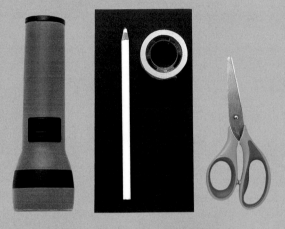

1 Place the torch on the sheet of card so that you can draw around the front side of it. Using the pencil, draw carefully around the torch.

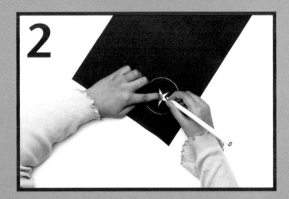

2 To make a star-shaped stencil, draw a star on paper and cut it out. Place the stencil in the torch-shape and draw around it.

3 Using the pair of scissors, carefully cut out both shapes. You should now be left with card that has a star shape in the middle.

4

Use sticky tape to fix the card to the front of the torch. Switch off all the lights and shine the torch to see your star in the sky. For something different, try cutting out a shape of the Moon.

Watch the Moon

Find the craters!
Not only are there craters on the surface of the Moon, but over a month, our nearest neighbour also changes shape. On a clear night, use binoculars to look for the Moon's craters. Never look at the Sun with binoculars as this will damage your eyes.

Whenever you see the Moon, whether at night or during the day, draw its shape on the correct date in a calendar. After a few months, your calendar will show you how the Moon goes through a series of changes (called phases).

Crazy comets

Finding new comets

New comets are discovered every year, but most of them are too faint to see without binoculars or a telescope.

1

To make big bits of space dust, place two digestive biscuits on a plate. Using the wooden spoon, crush the biscuits into large pieces.

You will need
- 2 large dinner plates
- Digestive biscuits
- Wooden spoon
- Hundreds and thousands
- Teaspoon
- Chocolate sprinkles
- Ice-cream scoop
- Chocolate ice-cream
- Ice-cream cone

2

To make smaller bits of space dust, add a large handful of hundreds and thousands to the crushed biscuits.

3

For extra space dirt, add two handfuls of chocolate sprinkles to the mixture. Use a teaspoon to give the space dust a good stir.

4

For the comet's head, use an ice-cream scoop to make a ball of ice-cream. Cover the ball of ice-cream in the dust mixture.

6

To make the comet's tail, carefully place the ice-cream ball onto an ice-cream cone. Push down lightly on the top of the ball to secure it.

5

Roll the ice-cream back into a ball-shape. If the ice-cream has started to melt, put it on another plate in the freezer.

Although you would never be able to eat a real comet, such as Hale-Bopp, this one is made from delicious ice-cream, so it tastes great!

Glossary

Asteroid – a chunk of rock that circles the Sun between the orbits of Jupiter and Mars

Astronaut – someone who travels into space

Astronomer – a scientist who studies the stars and space

Atmosphere – a mixture of gases around a planet

Cliff – a steep, high edge of land

Comet – an object that is made from ice, rocks and gas with a shining tail. Like a planet it orbits the Sun.

Crater – a wide hole caused by something crashing into the ground or by volcanic activity

Desert – a very dry area of land where hardly anything grows

Earthquake – an earth movement that causes the ground to shake and crack

Erupt – when a volcano erupts, it throws out hot lava and ash

Force – a pushing or pulling action that alters the movement or shape of an object

Gravity – the force that pulls objects such as the Sun, planets or moons towards each other

Meteorite – the remaining part of a meteoroid which falls to Earth

Meteoroid – a piece of rock that travels through space and burns brightly when it enters the Earth's atmosphere

Moon – the object that moves around the Earth, seen as a bright circle or crescent in the sky at night. Some other planets have moons.

Myth – a made-up story

Planet – a massive spherical object that orbits a star. For example, Earth orbits the Sun.

Ridge – a long, narrow piece of high land

Rusty – describes the red colour caused by iron reacting with air and water

Sunspot – a dark, irregular patch on the surface of the Sun

Tapestry – artwork embroidered on a piece of heavy cloth

Volcano – a mountain with openings at the top where lava and gas escape

Voyage – a long journey

Parent and teacher notes

This book includes material that would be particularly useful in helping to teach children aged 7–11 many elements of the English and Science curricula. These include the topic of Earth and space. It also provides opportunities for cross-curricular lessons, especially those involving Geography, History and Art.

Extension activities

Writing
Each double-page information spread has a title, introduction and three paragraphs of text, each with its own sub-heading.

1) On page 6 the planets are listed. 'My Very Educated Mother Just Served Us Noodles' is a silly sentence that will help you to remember them in order from the Sun. This is because the initial letters match up. Can you make up a sentence in reverse, starting with N for Neptune?

2) Use the information in this book to create a table giving facts about all the planets in our universe so that they can be compared. Use headings such as size, features, etc.

3) Make up your own space travel diary using the information in this book. Describe your journey and what you think it would feel like living on the different planets.

4) Choose a period in history and imagine you are there, watching a comet. Write about what you think it is. What does it look like? What would you do?

Speaking and listening
Page 24 mentions martians. Work with a partner and act out a conversation with a friendly alien. Change their character to be curious, war-like, excited, or tired from their journey.

Science
The topic of the Earth, Sun, planets and stars relates to the study of our solar system. It also relates to the topics of forces (p8 – gravity as a force, p20 – how do rockets get into space? and p43 – coping with no gravity); light (pp9, 10, 11 and 19 – including why we have day

and night) and the interdependence of life on Earth (pp16–17).

Study the night sky with binoculars or a telescope. Can you find the Milky Way (our galaxy) and can you see any constellations (groups of stars that make a picture). There are 88 of them!

Page 10 warns about the danger of looking at the Sun or spending too long in the Sun. Investigate the ozone layer, which filters out harmful UV rays. Write a short report of what you find.

Cross-curricular links
1) Geography: Page 8 shows how the Earth orbits the Sun every year. How does this link with our seasons? Why is it summer in the UK when it is winter in Australia? Find out how much of Earth is covered by seas or fresh water. Which areas of the land are inhabited, and which are not? Why do you think this is?

2) History: Page 12 features the Roman god Mercury. Research other Roman gods and find modern uses of their names.

Pages 20 (the first person on the Moon) and 42 (the first person in space) record two major events in space exploration. Write a newspaper-style report on either of them as if they had just happened.

Using the projects
Children can follow or adapt these projects at home. Here are some ideas for extending them:

Page 44: Research some examples of constellations. Copy or trace a constellation pattern and glue it to a sheet of black paper. Put the paper on a soft surface such as thick cardboard or the carpet and carefully push a hole through each dot with a pin. Hold the paper to the light to see your constellation.

Page 45: How does your Moon calendar match up with our yearly calendar? Do the cycles of the Moon match our months?

Page 46: Design and make other space-themed food, shaped like a rocket, planet or alien. How do astronauts eat? Design and make a food for them.

Did you know?

- Despite being the closest planet to the Sun, Mercury is not the warmest. Venus is warmer. Mercury is one of the coldest planets in the Solar System. This is because it has no atmosphere to trap heat.

- Asteroids that cross the orbit of the Earth as they move around the Sun are called Apollo asteroids. Scientist believe that an Apollo asteroid could have hit Earth about 65 million years ago, causing the dinosaurs to become extinct.

- Some people believe that, one day, astronauts may travel to and live on Mars. Mars is more like Earth than any other planet: it has volcanoes, polar ice caps, climatic seasons and clouds.

- Meteorites have been known to kill livestock and damage houses and cars.

- The same side of the Moon always faces the Earth. This means that we never see the other side.

- The pressure is so great on Jupiter that anything entering its atmosphere would be crushed immediately, including a spacecraft.

- One year on Jupiter is equal to twelve years on Earth.

- Neptune is the fourth largest planet in the Solar System. It is big enough to fit 60 Earths inside.

- Jupiter is so massive that if it were hollow, all of the other planets would fit inside it.

- When the Earth enters a meteoroid stream left by a comet it produces a meteor shower. These showers can be predicted and come every year or so. The meteor showers can be quite spectacular, involving over 100 meteors an hour.

- Violent storms occur on Saturn, some with winds up to 1,770 kilometres per hour!

- Early astronomers believed that the dark patches on the surface of the Moon were oceans.

- Astronauts need to be tied to their beds when they are asleep in space so that they do not float away.

- Without the Sun life on Earth would not exist. It would be so cold that no living thing would be able to survive and our planet would be completely frozen.

- Uranus is about four times as large as the Earth and fifteen times as heavy.

- Mars has seasons similar to our planet, but they last much longer. For example, summer on Mars lasts 199 Earth days.

- Without a spacesuit, an astronaut's blood would boil in space!

- It takes Uranus 84 years to make one orbit of the Sun. It would always be your birthday on Uranus. There is only a single day and night every year.

- Venus spins 'backwards', so the Sun rises in the west and sets in the east.

- Venus is the brightest planet in the Earth's night sky. Only the Moon (which is not a planet) is brighter. Venus outshines the other planets because its thick clouds reflect the Sun's light.

- In space, astronauts are up to 5 centimetres taller than they are on Earth. There is less gravity pushing down on their backbone in space, so it stretches. As soon as the astronauts return to Earth, their height goes back down to what it was before.

Solar System quiz

The answers to these questions can all be found by looking back through the book. See how many you get right. You can check your answers on page 56.

1) How many days does it take for the Earth to go around the Sun?
   A – 365
   B – 12
   C – 1

2) Nights on Mercury are:
   A – Extremely hot
   B – Bitterly cold
   C – Stormy

3) Water, warmth from the Sun and what else is needed to make life on Earth possible?
   A – Acid
   B – Volcanoes
   C – Air

4) What is Earth's closest neighbour in space?
   A – Venus
   B – The Moon
   C – Jupiter

5) What colour is Mars?
   A – Blue
   B – Green
   C – Red

6) Jupiter is very…
   A – Hot
   B – Small
   C – Stormy

7) What is Uranus's largest moon called?
   A – Titania
   B – Tracey
   C – Titanic

8) How many different types of plants and animals are there on Earth?
   A – More than thirty million
   B – More than twenty million
   C – More than ten million

9) Halley's Comet returns every:
   A – 100 years
   B – 45 years
   C – 76 years

10) What is a meteorite?
   A – A meteor that lands on Earth
   B – A meteor that lands on the Moon
   C – A meteor that breaks up in space

11) Which planet is the stormiest?
   A – Earth
   B – Uranus
   C – Neptune

12) An asteroid is…
   A – A failed planet
   B – A failed star
   C – Another Sun

Find out more

Books to read

Exploring Our Solar System by John Farndon, Heinemann Library, 2010

Navigators – Stars and Planets by Dr Mike Goldsmith, Kingfisher, 2008

Our Solar System and Beyond by Peter Riley, Franklin Watts, 2008

Planets by Charlotte Guillian, Heinemann Library, 2009

Solar System by Emily Bone, Usborne Publishing Ltd, 2010

Places to visit

The Spaceguard Centre, Knighton
www.spaceguarduk.com
Take a look through Wales's biggest telescope and see what stars you can spot. Come and see all the equipment used to observe space. You will also learn about Spaceguard and what they do to raise public awareness of comet and asteroid impacts.

National Space Centre, Leicester
www.spacecentre.co.uk
Take a journey through the six hands-on galleries, stopping at over 150 interactive experiences. Travel in the glass lifts in the 42-metre high Rocket Tower. Visit the museum at night and you can look at the stars close up.

Royal Observatory, London
www.rmg.co.uk
A variety of interesting astronomy-related films are being shown on the new digital laser planetarium projector. You will be able to take a look at the Earth and Solar System from space and explore the stars and galaxies of our universe.

Euro Space Center, Belgium
www.eurospacecenter.be/envisit.htm
Experience a full-scale mock-up of the American space shuttle and experience some of the feelings a real astronaut would experience in space. Meet an astronaut and hear stories and experiences of working and living in space. Learn about all the training they have to go through before visiting space.

Websites

www.kidsastronomy.com
Learn about the Solar System, the planets and moons with facts, diagrams and interesting animations.

www.nationalgeographic.com/kids
Find out how the Solar System began, with facts and videos. You can test your knowledge afterwards with a fun quiz.

www.sciencemuseum.org.uk
A website for all aspects of science. Visit the online space section and take a look at the stories timeline. Learn about space missions that will take place in the future.

www.nasa.gov/audience/forkids/kidsclub/flash/index.html
At the NASA Kids' Club website, play lots of games involving space and the Solar System for all abilities.

Aldrin, Buzz 20
Armstrong, Neil 20
asteroids 7, 36, 52
astronauts 20, 21, 42, 43, 52, 53
Charon 35
comets 7, 38–39, 40, 46–47
craters 12, 19, 23, 30
Deimos 22
dwarf planets 7, 34, 35
Earth 6, 16–17, 18, 20, 34, 52, 53
Gagarin, Yuri 42
Galileo 27
Hale-Bopp 39, 47
Halley's comet 38
Hoba West 41
Jupiter 7, 26–27, 28, 36, 39, 52
Mars 6, 22–23, 24–25, 36, 52
martians 24, 25
Mercury 6, 9, 12–13, 27, 52
meteorites 41, 52
meteoroids 7, 40

meteors 40, 41
Miranda 30, 31
Moon 6, 18–19, 20–21, 45, 53
moons 6, 22, 27, 30, 31, 32, 35
Neptune 7, 28, 32–33, 36, 52
Phobos 22
Pluto 34–35
probes 24, 25, 29, 32, 37
prominences 11
Saturn 7, 28–29, 53
spacecraft 13, 15, 18, 42
Sun 6, 8, 10–11, 12, 14, 16, 18, 35, 38, 53
telescopes 27, 34, 46
Triton 32
Uranus 7, 28, 30–31, 53
Venus 6, 9, 14–15, 52, 53
volcanoes 14, 17, 23, 32, 52

Solar System quiz answers

1) A	7) A
2) B	8) A
3) C	9) C
4) B	10) A
5) C	11) C
6) C	12) A